MEDITATIONS ON
SEASCAPES AND CYPRESS

Poems by
Jennifer Lagier

BLUE LIGHT PRESS ◆ 1ST WORLD PUBLISHING

1ST WORLD
PUBLISHING

SAN FRANCISCO ◆ FAIRFIELD ◆ DELHI

Meditations on Seascapes and Cypress
Copyright ©2021 Jennifer Lagier

BLUE LIGHT PRESS
www.bluelightpress.com
bluelightpress@aol.com

1ST WORLD PUBLISHING
PO Box 2211
Fairfield, IA 52556
www.1stworldpublishing.com

BOOK & COVER DESIGN
Melanie Gendron
melaniegendron999@gmail.com

AUTHOR PHOTO
Laura Bayless

FIRST EDITION

Library of Congress Cataloging-in-Publication Data

ISBN: 978-1-4218-3687-4

Meditations on Seascapes and Cypress

"May your trails be crooked, winding,
lonesome, dangerous, leading to the most amazing view.
May your mountains rise into and above the clouds."

— *Edward Abbey*

Table of Contents

White Fire of the Stars 1

Full Moon Over Sausalito 2

Cloud Angel 3

Fall 4

Santa Lucias 5

Trail's End 6

Upper Fiscalini Ranch Trail 7

Smolder 8

Autumn Dunes 9

Marina Dunes Preserve 10

Harbor 11

Daguerreotype 12

Celestial Orb 13

Moonstone Beach 14

Moon Fall 15

Sand Bar 16

Descent 17

Beach Bon Mot 18

Harvest Moon 19

Blue Heron 23

Sentinel 24

Ripple Effect 25

Over the Moon 26

On the Verge 27

Leffingwell Landing 28

Fire in the Sky 29

Fog Walker 30

If Trees Could Talk 31

Atmospheric Disturbance 32

November Ramble 33

Brassy Backdrop 34

Moonstone Meander 35

Windbreak 36

Outlook 37

Misty Morning 38

Squall 39

Moonstone Beach Boardwalk Trail 40

Red Sky Morning 41

Spring Cleaning 45

Celebrants 46

Soar 47

Plummet 48

Nocturnal Sonata 49

Homecoming 50

Disappearing Act 51

Maelstrom 52

Epiphany 53

Storm 54

Rain Lullaby 55

Oxalis 56

Almond Blossoms and Bees 57

Storm Clouds and Lupine 58

Peach Blossoms 59

Bees 60

Central Valley Spring 61

Night Music 62

Monterey Marina 63

Spring Rainstorm 64

Escalon Sunrise 65

Low Tide 66

Wildflower Ramble 67

Gratitude 68

Postcards of Light 71

Scarlet Salvia Plunder 72

Anna's Hummingbirds 73

Naked Ladies 74

Under White Fingers of the Moon 75

Mantilija Poppies 76

Ocean Fog 77

Squirrel 78

Mist, Moon and Cypress 79

Frog Pond 80

Solstice Moon 81

Wetland Cypress 82

Cambria Ramble 83

Thistle 84

Sunset at Leffingwell Landing 85

Moonstone Morning 86

Drizzle 87

Camera Obscura 88

Del Monte Beach 89

Morning Hike 90

Acknowledgements 92

About the Author 95

Books by Jennifer Lagier 97

Fall

"*A kestrel can and does hover in the dead calm of summer days, when there is not the faintest breath of wind. He will, and does, hover in the still, soft atmosphere of early autumn, when the gossamer falls in showers, coming straight down as if it were raining silk.*"

— *Richard Jefferies*

White Fire of the Stars

Title from "Sleeping in the Forest" by Mary Oliver

A refugee mountain lion
creeps across steepled roof,
onto patio, over fence,
sets my dogs barking,
awakens neighbors at 2 a.m.

Stealthy cougar slinks,
a liquid blur between hibiscus,
roses, Pride of Madeira,
captured mid-prowl
by security camera.

Possums, skunks, feral cats
sense its threatening trespass,
vanish into burrows,
observe from shadows.

From oak limbs, nocturnal owls croon.
Panther prowls, sniffs the air,
white fire from distant stars overhead.

Full Moon Over Sausalito

"and in its shadow we know one another"
— W.S. Merwin, "The Rock"

Swollen orange luminosity
ascends from inky sea,
hangs above Berkeley hills,
spills jagged gold ribbon
across crinkled water.

Silver strung Bay Bridge
sutures San Francisco
to hulking Marin headlands,
invites sailboats
into drowsy marina.

We saunter through shadows,
entranced by lunar resurrection,
admire egg yolk moon,
shimmering starlight,
firefly skyline.

Cloud Angel

"I am a feather on the bright sky"
— N. Scott Momaday, from "The Delight Song of Tsoai-talee"

Shore fog molds itself into a winged seraph
sailing across sapphire sky
above shaggy pines.

Gray pelicans soar, skim autumn ocean,
survey pleated waves,
belly-flop into anchovy shoals.

A sea gull, masquerading as spirit guide,
spirals over damp beach, drops a feather token,
leaves an angelic fragment behind.

Fall

Indian summer wanes.
Blazing foliage expires,
drops from bare limbs.
Orange and gold shrouds,
ghosts of past seasons,
litter fog-dampened ground.

Marigold embers turn into ash.
Fading geraniums yellow and shrivel.
Chill winds slash ashore,
spread exploded puffballs'
feathery suicide seed.

Daylight diminishes.
Icy night replaces blue sky
with yawning black heaven.
Frigid lunar orb rises, releases
squeaky bats, primal fears
as emerging stars glitter.

Sirius, the winter sparkler,
brilliant white with a touch of sapphire,
flickers against inky universe.
Infinite galaxies of stellar remnants
signal the end of summer's dog days.

Santa Lucias

"By evening, the women are mountains
wrapped in dark shawls."
— Maya Khosla

At daybreak, Ventana Wilderness reveals
slow-healing wildfire scars.
Sunrise snags scarlet petticoats
on rounded blue hills, drifting lavender fog.

Golden mountain range
shawled with Spanish-mossed oaks
conceals redwood groves,
icy springs, shaded fields of sorrel.

Bohemian writers and musicians
congregate in off-road communes
among cypress, hard-scrabble slopes.

By noon, woodpeckers hammer insects
from dead, crumbling pines.
Hawks spiral above jagged cliffs.
Stellar jays scatter into ragged sequoias.
Blackbirds stretch glossy feathers.

After sunset, the sisterhood gathers
in a pulsing drum circle.
Big Sur women share stories, chants,
whirl around wanton flames.

Trail's End

"sound of inner stone with heart on fire"
— W.S. Merwin, "The Rock"

To my right, frothy breakers
fracture crumbling boulders
along Moonstone Beach.
Sullen clouds hug ragged shore.

On the left, cautious jackrabbits
forage among petrified thistles.
A cacophony of competing fragrances
from sage and pine overwhelm.

Ancient cypress and dusty oaks
groan in fog-instigated breeze,
shift Spanish moss shrouds,
spill gray squirrels, squawking jays.

Is trail's end my choice of destination
or pre-ordained by some wry acrobatic of fate?
As golden sunrise ignites willow thicket,
I discover all paths take me to the same place.

Upper Fiscalini Ranch Trail

"I have seen them when there was nothing else."
— W.S. Merwin, "The Hands"

Overconfidence seduces me onto vertical footpath.
Skunk reek permeates forest essence,
eclipses sun-released pine perfume.
Flying Wallenda squirrels soar between tree limbs,
but gravity tugs at arthritic knees.

As September tapers to a close,
I enter my seventh decade,
replenish the soul's depleted pantry,
stockpile starburst sunrises, lavender twilight
to illuminate coming winter's dark days.

I ascend dry grass ridge line,
survey restless ocean, cymbal waves
as they percuss against broken shore,
pause frequently to scribble word sketches
of scarlet poison oak, cobalt stellar jays.

Smolder

Joggers plod toward splayed piers,
inscribe sunken prints upon unblemished strand.

Cormorants skitter across Leffingwell Landing
as tourists scavenge moonstones,
search for holy grail snails.

Muddled sky spills muted sunlight,
seagulls, lacy drizzle.

Receding tide relinquishes silver driftwood,
shattered scallop shells, macraméd kelp.

Recursive waves whisper ashore,
deconstruct granite, churn breeding sediment,
augment rising seas.

Mist simmers among rogue eucalyptus.
Foamy surf rushes, overwhelms glowing sand.

Earth patiently erases, reconstructs jagged shoreline,
disregards passing time.

Autumn Dunes

Indian summer succumbs to cool morning mist.
Sun burnt chaparral flaunts scarlet, maroon.
Pearly everlasting outlasts green foliage,
displays autumnal gold.
Red berries appear among drying ruins.
Sticky monkey overshadows silvery sage.

I approach September's familiar portal,
traverse a threshold of seven decades on earth.
Ahead, gray fog delivers delicate drizzle,
melds with low clouds, sullen ocean.
Moving slowly, with care for aching bones,
I contemplate coming finale, dawning unknown.

Marina Dunes Preserve

Morning surf corrugates,
crashes ashore,
scatters dismembered kelp
against etch-a-sketch sands.

Ground squirrels scamper across ice plant hollow,
squat atop fallen cypress.
Gliding hawks survey chaparral
as shredded fog drifts overhead.

Cottontails shelter beneath white sage
as field mice forage among golden dunes.
I meditate, perched upon rickety bench.
Within a eucalyptus grove, blue jays frisk brittle grass.

Harbor

Empty yachts fringe weathered piers,
silently float upon tranquil water.

Ship masts mimic a nautical forest,
flutter red and yellow flags.

Harbor seals break the surface
of taut bay, vie for dry boulders.

Blackbirds and gulls spiral above anchored ships,
capricious scraps of feathered confetti.

Morning quiet mingles with hanging mist.
Power-walking the empty trail, I am the solitary explorer.

Daguerreotype

Silent rows of fishing boats float
upon bronze-tinted water.
Rocking masts scrape orange and gray
brightening sky, offer convenient perch
for blackbirds, mouthy gulls
who taunt passing walkers.

Sleepy harbor seals
litter slippery rocks as
a lone otter drifts between piers,
dismantles black mussels.
Smell of coffee, frying bacon
spirals from shipboard galleys.

Golden beach gives back
ebbing tide rivulets, reveals
cast-ashore kelp,
an abandoned tennis shoe,
scattered encampments
of shivering homeless.

Celestial Orb

Lunar pearl floats above wetland pond,
hovers between black lace silhouettes,
shadow portraits of cypress.

Provocateur moon emboldens
nocturnal skunks and raccoons,
arouses passion in frustrated lovers.

Changing tide whispers suggestive innuendo
to stone-exposed shore as hanging orb
reveals mating harbor seals, silvery otters.

Moonstone Beach

Sleek gulls
streak colorless sky.
Distant fog smudges
uncertain horizons.

A small boy
gouges wet sand,
leaves weeping holes
along low-tide seashore.

Pelicans belly-flop
from thin summer air,
scoop wriggling silver
from wrinkled green ocean.

Surf sculpted adobe
leers from eroded cliffs
like a Neanderthal clan
of primitive totems.

I wander damp gravel,
crunch bulbous kelp,
remember stolen kisses,
consider my options.

Moon Fall

Silent morning, dark sky barely starting to color.
Moon fragment floats between cypress trunks,
disappears behind sand dunes, slides into ocean.

This is my quiet time, productive solitude
before rumble of passing cars, keening hawks,
children calling when neighbors waken.

Fingers transcribe what the muse whispers.
Metaphor raises a cautious head.
Poetry sneaks out from under thin shadows.

Sand Bar

Shadows fracture tide pool, white shore,
bisect low tide's exposed strand.

An arching cypress limb masquerades
as leaping harbor seal, curling dolphin.

Drifting mist, propelled by breeze,
cascades between granite monoliths.

Fog evaporates; morning sun ascends.
Silhouettes come into sharper focus.

Pelican pen and ink studies
tattoo pallid sand.

Descent

Roots of a wind-warped cypress
insinuate themselves into crevices
of succulent cloaked granite.

Weathered stairs angle in louvered descent
from dun-hued adobe bluff trail
to storm-exposed bedrock slabs.

Piled driftwood forms a flimsy shelter,
shields a huge sand-sculpted peace symbol
outlined by filigree of broken clam shells.

Like worn shoreline, we persevere,
hang on and endure, survive what bashes,
leaves scars, hidden remnants of hope.

Beach Bon Mot

"Whales," a driftwood message
etched into sand
exposed by low tide.

Passersby marvel at
the spectacle of mother humpback
and her frisky calf
as they breach and blow
just beyond rocky shore.

Outside protected cove,
the disturbed ocean boils.
Migrating leviathans
spout umbrella spume,
lift giant fins, smirking grins,
roll above curling surf.

Harvest Moon

Golden sycamore leaves
loosen from branches.
Indian Summer ignites
and hot weather lingers.

Harvest moon hangs in humid sky.
Open windows fail to capture
even the tiniest breeze.
Everyone simmers.

Late peaches swell and grow crimson.
An exhausted year pauses.
Pumpkins, almonds, ripened souls
prepare to be gathered.

Winter

"Winter is a season of recovery and preparation."
— Paul Theroux

Blue Heron

A giant blue heron strides
through shoreline shallows,
heaves himself aloft
into morning air above
sandy beach, tranquil tide pools.

Tiny white egrets forage
among exposed anemones,
green and mauve seaweed,
crack speared snails against stone,
extract tender morsels.

Wind and waves
sequence nature's stories
with a Zen soundtrack.
Painter, poet, photographer
capture unfolding dramas.

A dolphin aquacade
entertains crass crows
who gossip
from ringside seats
upon twisted cypress.

Sentinel

A scrap of Artemis floats
above filigree limbs,
hangs in icy sky
between witchy branches.
Anorexic moon dwindles
to white, glowing rib.

In the house beneath ancient oak,
human deconstruction persists —
relentless slide into dementia.
Names of objects, familiar recipes,
sense of time vanish,
family history erased.

Night is chill, growing darker.
Sinister storm clouds
coagulate overhead.

Ripple Effect

Tuxedoed geese waltz across still estuary.
Their graceful wakes pleat the dark water.

Unleashed dogs gallop along Del Monte Beach.
Red-faced owners jog in futile pursuit.

Grouchy harbor seals rumble, battle for sunlight,
push each other off sinking piers into icy bay.

At the intersection, a homeless woman
holds up a sign. I hand her ten dollars.

Walkers with coffee mugs smile and wave.
Winter morning seems warmer.

Over the Moon

"Beneath a sky thrown open
To the need of stars
To know themselves against the dark."
　　—*Joy Harjo, "Seven Generations"*

Full moon above bare oak branches.
Tiny diamonds burn through onyx firmament,
spill silver meteors.

Calla lilies
thrust pointy green pokers
unfold white flagons, collect crystal droplets
from moist evening mist.

Luminescence floods midnight garden,
where a glittery-eyed possum hisses
before she squeezes beneath picket fence.

Whirling spatter of streaking stars
revolves around celestial lunar spotlight,
its rainbow halo pulsing muted colors
toward slumbering earth.

On the Verge

"Return to the quiet edge, those private places."
— *Barbara Swift Brewer*

Frost-scalded, comb-over ice plant
straggles across bald, sloping sand.
Silver boardwalk sutures dunes,
rime glitter at sunrise.

Above turquoise breakers
shedding spindrift tatters,
a chevron of brown pelicans
patrol curving bay.

Dawn divulges a technicolor epiphany.
Kelp and flotsam, stirred by wind,
distract lone woman walker who pauses,
explores purple statice, brittle sage clusters.

Pink light pulses, emanates from chill horizon,
the ephemeral edge of earth's curvature,
gold-streaked sky, icy dunes,
muscular ocean.

Leffingwell Landing

White water chips away worn layers of dun adobe.
Defrosting boardwalk drips into gaping squirrel burrows.
A heron parks on a boulder, monitors passing anchovies.

Surf booms against crumbling shoreline.
I pause at earth's edge, year's end,
contemplate coming upheavals and losses.

Vigilant pelicans skid above El Niño spindrift.
Defiant ice plant clings to stone wreckage.
Rising sun illuminates shifting tide.

Fire in the Sky

Downpour empties overhead clouds,
leaves illumined husks
blazing against purple sky
during transient sunrise.

Cypress silhouettes call attention
to celestial fire-play as drifting fog
and stratocumulus merge,
provide a pink and gold light show.

Shape shifters morph, fleetingly glow,
fade to gray, brief radiance erased
by smudged thunderheads,
grumbling, incoming storm.

Fog Walker

Foggy morning folds around me
as I traverse wood chip trail.
A squirrel scales lanky pine,
clings to poison oak.

Mist suffuses ancient forest,
drips from twisted silvery limbs.
In golden meadow, a wild rabbit
sits up, startled by my appearance,
disappears in tall rattlesnake grass.

At ridge top, under broken cypress,
I rest on a dolphin bench,
savor isolation, accept serenity,
feel a higher power descend.

If Trees Could Talk

*"Trees are the earth's endless effort
to speak to the listening heaven."*
— *Rabindranath Tagore*

Crumpled cypress at earth's end complain
of lacerating winds, an icy fog
that cancels sun, consumes rocky headlands.

Coastal oaks communicate ancient truths,
bear their silvery scars like scabby
badges of resilience.

Above seer valley floor,
Monterey pines implore a higher power to intercede,
protect them from beetles and fire.

Eucalyptus semaphore
fragrant distress, their flayed bark,
sickle leaves, one-way tickets to heaven.

Atmospheric Disturbance

Full moon seeps through skylights,
illuminates squinty possums,
instigates arthritic agony,
keeps us tossing and turning.

In silent kitchen — chilly shadows.
Power failure extinguishes civilization,
leaves us with useless coffee pot,
cold cookware, shivery breakfast.

Revolutionary rumblings
thunder from hysterical headlines.
Tile floor crawls with displaced refugees,
proliferating dark ant invasion.

Outside, impaled oak tree saplings convulse
on their stakes, animated by slashing wind,
atmospheric river, bouncing pellets
of white, frozen rain.

November Ramble

As mercury plummets,
shocked grapevines turn crimson.
Summer's annuals blacken and shrivel.
Maples cast off ragged leaves.

Pets refuse to leave warm blankets.
Humans demonstrate faulty judgement,
wrap themselves in jackets and scarves,
meander along blue bay, chilly beach.

Cold wind pinches noses and fingers,
makes arthritic bones ache.
Shivering walkers stamp numb feet,
exhale pallid vapors, trudge winding trail.

Wan sunrise fails to thaw
or drive icy winter away.
Daylight dwindles.
Frost crust sparkles.

Brassy Backdrop

Sunset oozes
between arthritic oak limbs.
Squirrels chase one another
up and down gnarled trunks,
adorn angular branches.

I wander vacant sidewalk,
admire neighbors' window displays,
holiday decorations and lights.
Leashed dogs impatiently tug me
toward their favorite haunts.

Above us, gold gives way
to pulsing lavender,
charcoal-edged rain clouds.
Full moon floats over agitated bay
through purple layers of fog.

Moonstone Meander

Lavender fog
hangs above icy water.
Hoarfrost lingers,
preserved within shadow.

Joggers and dog walkers
share slanted boardwalk,
salute passersby
with cups of hot coffee.

Mobile meditation
erases white noise distractions.
While my soul breathes,
full moon's swollen tide
corrodes brittle shores.

Windbreak

Tenacious cypress anchor living windbreak,
detain shreds of traveling mist,
spill miniature diamonds.

As rough squalls rage,
walkers traverse a protective tunnel
that rebuffs sandblasting zephyrs.

Through an intersection of twisted limbs,
vignettes of spindrift, frenzied spume.
Sailboats yaw, tack across jagged surf.

Outlook

Dim morning —
dingy fogbanks mimic surf,
mist breakers billowing inland.

Egrets forage along rocky shore,
gaunt specters cloaked
within salty vapor.

A rough bench rooted
beneath ancient cypress
invites repose, meditation.

Smirking pelicans soar
majestically above silver waves,
offer mute epiphany.

I scribble poetry fragments,
seize freighted images
from soggy surroundings.

Misty Morning

Shredded fog drifts inland,
shrouds walking trail,
drips rhinestones
from contorted cypress.

Beach combers materialize
then vanish like wraiths
as mist swaddles
tide pools and shoreline.

Somewhere, morning sun rises,
lifts silvery vapor from wetlands.
Distant geese keen
from within chill miasma.

Squall

Atmospheric disturbance seethes just offshore,
paints sunset amber, charcoal and crimson.

Blackbirds sense approaching storm,
bolt food scraps,
seek shelter in scrub brush.

Evening walkers have second thoughts,
dig out Wellingtons, rain gear, umbrellas.

The first spatters glisten
against wooden deck, silver concrete.

Gigantic surf hammers beach and bluff,
incoming muscular squall.

Moonstone Beach Boardwalk Trail

Sparkling frost gilds planks.
Squirrels forego icy mornings,
hibernate deep underground.

Alongside Moonstone Beach,
pelicans pluck small fish,
float on silver lagoon.

Sun clears golden willows,
illuminates jagged ridge line, distant oaks,
blackbird sprinkled bog.

Red Sky Morning

Chill sunrise flares over wetlands,
vernal ponds,
jagged frame of dark cypress.

Silver linings blush pink.
Gold ignites far horizon.

Approaching storm front seethes,
spills charcoal clouds
against frosted sand dunes.

Icy wind shrieks inland from ocean.
Electricity charges surrounding air.
Spiraling hawks hang in technicolor sky.

Spring

"Everything is blooming most recklessly; if it were voices instead of colors, there would be an unbelievable shrieking into the heart of the night."

— *Rainer Maria Rilke*

Spring Cleaning

"I have slept with my cheek against the earth."
— *Erin Rodoni*

During winter, neglected garden shrivels from frostbite.
This bright morning, I weed alyssum,
dewy miner's lettuce, expunge purple spurge,
snip dead wood from roses, hibiscus.

Buried under dormant hydrangeas,
trumpet face daffodils, scarlet tulips
burst through fusty collage
of blackened leaf compost.

Crocuses stir,
eager for a deep drink, fresh air,
warm blanket of sunlight.
Hyacinths bracket blue and yellow viola.

Obsessed with rescuing order from chaos,
I migrate indoors, redirect motivation, toss old papers,
revise a poem, meditate and revive,
rub walnut office desk with fragrant orange oil.

Celebrants

Hummingbirds whirr
between salvia bushes,
dodge darting bat silhouettes
during lavender twilight.
Camouflaged tree frogs
chorus a rousing bass beatbox.

In awakening flower beds,
purple crocus erupt.
Blind narcissus brandish green daggers.
Calla lilies unfurl,
virginal nuns beside ruddy vinca.
Entombed daffodils emerge,
flaunt yellow trumpets.

Sap rises, restores wizened limbs.
Plum tree buds crown,
explode into white and pink blossoms.
Persephone resurrects.

Soar

"The exit is a portal.
You must grow wings."
    — *Maxine Chernoff*

Scarlet hang-gliders mingle
with ashen-winged sea gulls,
coast on thermal currents,
skim scalloped rims of gold dunes.

Sunlight reanimates morning walkers,
thaws frozen fingers, numb toes.
Night's soggy drizzle
scours glowering fog remnants
as origami poppies unfold.

Oxalis punctuates sedge,
restores faith among the winter weary.
Bay trail winds through eucalyptus forest.
Day warms; Monarch butterflies soar.

Plummet

"I was a star falling from the night sky..."
— Joy Harjo

At the Garland Park star party,
amateur astronomers gather,
sip hot chocolate, scalding coffee, peppermint tea,
shiver despite down jackets.
Serenaded by crickets, they witness
the Geminid meteor shower.

Sparkling space debris
from the 3200 Phaeton asteroid
spatters the night sky
with 60 multicolored comets per hour.
Distant galaxies whirl
above cottonwoods, sycamore, pine trees.

Atmospheric friction fuels
a celestial light show.
Over-the-hill heavenly bodies,
like fading celebrities,
burn bright, then flame out.

Nocturnal Sonata

"You must be friends with silence to hear."
— *Joy Harjo*

Aroused by percussive rainfall,
a tree frog warbles his private sonata.
Amphibian troubadours join night's symphony,
croon a Zen coda.

In sleeping cottage, a tabby
purrs beside whispering fire.
Owls perched on twisted oak branches
hoot a territorial chorus.

Ring-tailed ninja racoons
emerge from storm drains,
sift through whirling debris
in roaring waterfall gutters.

Aging house creaks, settles, grumbles.
Gas wall heater whooshes.
I float mutely into melodic dreams
through silver curtains of downpour.

Homecoming

"What a long time the place was empty even in my sleep."
— W.S. Merwin

Dreams return me to the rose-entwined porch
of a forgotten seaside bungalow
sandwiched between steepled Victorians,
white clapboard womb with baby blue shutters.

Purple morning glories wind themselves
from crumbly soil to shingled roof.
Green runners clutch aluminum rain spout
with sticky leprechaun fingers.

Pink and lavender hydrangeas
form an eclectic pointillist mural,
mingle with fiery marigolds,
creamy foxgloves, cobalt lobelia.

A gray tabby purrs
over a welcoming threshold.
Within the serene kitchen, I take root,
brew a fragrant pot of Moroccan mint tea.

Disappearing Act

"You know how it feels,
wanting to walk into
the rain and disappear…"
    — Mary Oliver, "At Blackwater Pond"

Winter dissolves into snapdragons,
purple viola, pink hyacinth
aroused by May showers.

Fog banks kamikaze
against jagged Monterey pines,
spiral inland behind stony hills
to reveal egg yolk sunshine.

The poinsettia sluffs spent petals.
I sweep cobwebs from windows and eaves,
replenish winter's petrified topsoil,
divide bearded iris.

Summer shoves rain clouds
east toward snow crusted Sierras
as last season's daffodils crumble to compost.
Marigolds and zinnias splatter the backyard —
orange, red and gold fireworks.

Maelstrom

Storm wind screams inland,
skims spindrift from raging surf,
rips apart oak trees, cypress,
shatters golden acacias.

Malevolent clouds spill icy torrent.
Like prehistoric cave dwellers,
we shelter from deluge
near a sputtering fire.

Atmospheric river rampages
through rocky canyons,
un-shingles rooftops,
floods sodden valley.

Epiphany

Sunrise simmers among thunderheads,
above frayed cypress, splintered oaks,
shattered Monterey pines.

Overnight, brittle grasses plump,
regain emerald coloring,
absorb silver rain and revive.

I walk quietly, startle morning sparrows,
consider subtle heartbeat of distant surf.
My nourished soul soars.

Storm

"I meant to live a quiet life."
— Mary Oliver

Wind gusts across Pacheco Pass,
riles muddy reservoir water,
gnaws red volcanic shore.
Deluge transforms barren hills
into lush emerald velvet.

Overhead, storm clouds split,
deliver silver payload.
Swollen creek spills
beyond melting riverbank,
circles leafless sycamores,
inundates sodden pasture.

Gold bleeds through engorged thunderheads.
Sun lasers jagged blue mountain tops,
illuminates expanding puddles
with smears of intense yellow mustard.

Rain Lullaby

... All night
I rose and fell, as if in water...
— Mary Oliver, "Sleeping in the Forest"

Too much of a good thing
pours from bruised, freighted clouds.
Silver snipes glistening shingles,
batters snapdragons, flattens sweet-peas.
Puddles overwhelm sodden ground.

I dream of drowning,
irrigation water rising from bare feet to waist,
trapped in a cement-lined ditch
with unscalable walls.

Wind-driven deluge brings back Cape Flattery,
winter slush pelting trailer house windows,
hail encrusting nasturtiums, frozen succulents,
sleet turning to snow.

Tonight's rain dwindles, whispers lullabies,
memories of peat-darkened Middle River.
Within the teak-planked womb
of my old fishing boat, Ms. As Is,
I rock peacefully beneath Delta starlight.

Oxalis

False shamrocks cluster
among purple lupine,
wild alyssum, gold poppies.

Bermuda buttercup
and goat's foot sour grass
were once aphrodisiacs
used by native Algonquins.

They announce spring's arrival,
the heat waves
of premature summer.

Free-spirited oxalis
invade marshy wetlands,
punctuate cypress shadows
with bright yellow faces.

Almond Blossoms and Bees

Popcorn blooms erupt from branches,
spill like powdered sugar
on almond orchard floor,
mimic faux snow drifts,
exude sweet aroma.

Bees cluster,
peer inside kitchen window,
trail me outside as I
wander from tree to tree,
capturing spring
with notebook and camera.

Against bridal backdrop
of pink-tinged, falling petals,
endangered pollinators
fill the air with humming,
caress swollen stamens,
pilfer pollen.

Storm Clouds and Lupine

During the brief window
between storm fronts,
I take my bored dogs to the wetlands,
where we explore battered tules,
mud-puddled trails,
flowering meadow.

Amber poppies
accent gray sage,
saturated foxtails.
Short-lived sunshine
gilds splintered cypress,
lavender lupine.

Wet dogs sashay
though soggy fiddleneck,
drag me in futile pursuit
of velvety brown squirrels,
fleeing frenetic sparrows.

Peach Blossoms

Eloquent limbs uplifted in fifth position.
Almond trunks pose en pointe.

Slender Degas ballerinas
unfurl light pink petals
against baby blue sky,
chiffon rain clouds.

Central Valley spring
delicately relevés
through Midas poppies,
azure lupine, canary mustard.

It's the season Persephone resurrects.
Hyacinths leap from earthy underworld,
purple blooms reaching toward heaven.

Bees

Despite overcast sky
and absence of blossoms,
bees emerge from stacked hives,
explore nearby garden.

With nothing to pollinate,
they stray from the orchard,
ignore immature almond buds,
buzz outside kitchen window.

They seek rogue sweetness,
stamens to fondle, flowers to pillage.

Curious avatars follow me
as I water potted azaleas.
They hum around my head,
a high-intensity halo.

Central Valley Spring

An explosive chaos of tree-toppling winds,
days of impenetrable fog.

Almond orchards seethe with courier bees.
Past-their-prime petals snow into drifts.

After dark months,
pastel pink bursts from bristling limbs,
promises summer sweetness,
peaches, crabapples, plums.

Night Music

Darkness devours lavender dusk.
Lunar orb hangs between ragged limbs.

Silver paints budding willows,
emerging lupines. Wetland pond —
a refracted gold trail.

Gentle song of crooning owl
harmonizes with muffled boom
of incoming surf.

A spooked cloud of squeaking bats
passes before blinking stars,
punctuates the night air.

Monterey Marina

Sunrays reach toward silver bay
through muddled layers of fog,
anchored sailboats,
harbor seals arched like parentheses
upon scattered rocks.

The homeless curl
among blooming wild lilacs
within nests of soiled blankets,
flattened circles of weeds.

Anglers come ashore
for steaming black coffee,
to refill propane canisters,
wash themselves in public showers
after days of wrestling with rodeo waves.

Tourists taste clam chowder samples,
splurge on postcards and saltwater taffy.
Street musicians busk at the entrance
to Fisherman's Wharf.

Ghosts of old Spanish mariners
linger within wooden effigies
in front of seafood restaurants,
gift shops, fish mongers
as they peddle their wares.

Spring Rainstorm

Silver sky oppresses
wind-blown almonds,
saturates dripping leaves.

Light shifts from charcoal
to acute golden clarity,
then opaque again.

Ravenous sparrows and crows
feed on drowning earthworms
as they writhe from wet ground.

Torn bits of storm-shredded ash trees
litter flooded sidewalk,
an extemporaneous mosaic upon sodden lawn.

Escalon Sunrise

Sunrise illuminates puddles
left by yesterday's rain.
Beehives rest, await morning light.

A plump dove scratches among storm detritus,
follows a glittery ribbon,
finds a breakfast of snails.

Fallen oranges soften, food for gnats.
Pummeled wisteria sheds purple tears.
Sodden almond trees lift branches
past dark clouds toward brightening sky.

Low Tide

Denim sky, sun,
a deceptive impression of warmth.

At 46 degrees, my huffing breath resembles
hookah clouds, masquerades as white smoke.

Turquoise ocean flings chilly, creamy surf
over jagged stones onto glistening beach.

Oxalis and poppies shiver,
encroach upon wild lilac trail.

Storms simmer below bright horizon.
Dolphins encircle surfers straddling boards.

Wildflower Ramble

Our footsteps bruise a dark trail
through foxtails, poppies, sky lupine.

Here among greasewood,
homesteads melt back to fern.
A sinking oak rots
into damp miner's lettuce.

Iron nails rust within tin filigree,
a termite bored trailer bed,
weather bowed axles.

Last winter's yarrow
bisects acres of mustard.
Sage interrupts yellow broom.
Lichen sprouts from stone fractures.

Frantic doves, stirred by trespass,
splash across fog-smudged skies,
spilling soft wakes of feathers,

as hawk shadows paint
rugged hills, redwood canyons,
wild radish meadows.

Gratitude

Praise sun etched cypress
lifting needled limbs
above white sage and driftwood,
low-tide exposed beach.

Walk in mindfulness along gentle trail
beside wrinkled ocean.
Pet passing dogs.
Dispense baked, tasty treats.

Meditate upon swooping pelicans,
golden-eyed heron,
trash-talking jays,
paranoid blackbirds.

Sit in silence
within a cathedral
of wind ruffled redwoods.
Feel higher power resurrect the soul,
heal your heart.

Bless this bright day.

Summer

"In the middle of winter, I discovered that an invincible summer is inside of me."

— *Albert Camus*

Postcards of Light

On weekends, we tied to bulrush berms
fringing Middle River's peat-darkened channel.
Without streetlights, celestial sapphire
stretched plush ether
above our small cabin cruiser.

Reclining against teak deck,
we pondered expansive summer night
on the San Joaquin Delta —
hypnotic silver moon, the rare shooting star,
sporadic asteroid showers.

Stellar messages we could not decipher
streaked across diamond pierced indigo,
then vanished over safflower fields.

Along swampy slough,
catfish splashed and bullfrogs rumbled.
Burning planetoids plummeted into dark corn rows.
For hours, we meditated upon the shimmering cosmos,
taut anchor line inscribing circular mandalas
upon onyx water.

Scarlet Salvia Plunder

*"During the brief week that the redbud blooms, the cardinal emerges
from its pink waves like Botticelli's Venus rising from the sea."*
— *Diane Porter*

Twilight hummingbirds scorn lavender spires,
plunge needle beaks deep,
extract sweetness from red salvia blooms.

Ruby-headed sprites hurtle among scarlet shrubs.
Fairy wings thrum as they hang in warm autumn air.
Plundered blossoms exude crushed herb perfume.

I watch them gorge, sample foxglove nectar,
rocket across starry sky,
dart beneath rising moon.

Anna's Hummingbirds

"Anna's Hummingbirds are a year-round resident in Monterey County. This tiny bird is common in open woodlands (especially areas with eucalyptus trees), sage chaparral and residential gardens."
— Pacific Grove Museum of Natural History

Tempestuous redheads
insert hypodermic beaks into pink lilies,
then careen among wild lilac, miniature roses,
high off sweet honey.

Black and gold bumblebees
ignore these erratic, iridescent sprites,
lazily buzz around Mexican sage,
plunge down chalice throats
of bronze bearded iris.

Tiny hummers whirr
toward scarlet salvia beacons,
seek fat spiders, circling gnats,
dive like a feathery battalion
of Delta Force choppers.

Naked Ladies

Each August, lilies rise from the dead.
Solo or en masse, naked ladies perform
an end-of-summer, erotic ballet.

Deceptively hardy, they thrive
when neglected, disregard frost,
shun over-watering, revel in drought.

Pink strumpets cavort along estuary,
define graveyard boundary,
fringe winding trail.

They congregate like a troupe
of brash chorus girls
within weed-overgrown vacant lots.

I admire their in-your-face tenacity,
audacious trumpet flower blooms,
spunky, sinewy stalks.

Under White Fingers of the Moon

from a poem by Russell Salamon

Fog wraiths resurrect from shuddering ocean,
drift inland to surround
ascendant lunar pearl against ebony cosmos,
chase huntress Diana and her starry hounds
across celestial prairie.

Night-blooming honeysuckle
dangles creamy fingers from intertwined vines.
Jasmine exudes erotic perfume.
As a snowy owl croons,
camouflaged crickets twitter.

Pale lovers embrace,
naked within shadows
beneath swollen full moon.

Mantilija Poppies

*"The Matilija's expansiveness makes it an ideal hillside plant. Their kooky
Dr. Seuss–meets–Blake attitudes benefit from distance."*
— *The Dry Garden*

Fried egg blooms thrive in barren canyons,
proliferate among dry washes,
overwhelm sage scrub, coast chaparral.

If size and audacity were considerations,
these twelve-inch blossoms with a Chumash name
would reign as California's state flower.

White poppies embellish burnt wilderness,
brash chorus girls ornamenting arid slopes,
unabashed exhibitionists.

Ocean Fog

My father called it Nature's air-conditioning,
drizzly vapor pulled ashore from the ocean,
drawn by hellish central valley heat,
more ethereal than tule fog,
winter months without sunlight.

From the deck at Nepenthe,
I watch mist rise, ghostly apparition
crawling inland, slowly effacing
blue Ventana wilderness mountain tops.

At the ranch outside Modesto,
mercury inches upward past 90.
Within cracked-earth orchards, temperatures sizzle.
It's 75 degrees along the coast in Big Sur,
where white-legged tourists
sprout goose bumps and shiver.

Squirrel

He carries scarlet flowers
stolen from decapitated primrose
in his mouth up a tree
to an invisible lover.

Earlier in the week,
my husband gifted me
with crimson roses
displayed with love
on our dining room table.

Human and squirrel share the mute urge
to express romantic impulses
with a grand floral gesture.

Mist, Moon and Cypress

Humid vapors levitate
above smoldering wetlands.
Restless ducks and stilts squawk and flutter.

Tree frog symphony
invokes Druidic rites,
turning tide, wind-propelled mist.

Artemis rises between lanky cypress,
illuminates drifting fog,
diffused glow against ebony sky.

Frog Pond

Watercress and floating leaves mingle
with reflected blue sky.

Mosquito fish dart from shadows,
nibble green pillows of algae.

Horsetail fern topples under pressure
from yesterday's rainfall.

Ducks forage among submerged
willows and tules.

Bullfrogs croak a solemn dirge,
invoke mutating progeny, wriggling tadpoles.

Solstice Moon

Night trembles
on the precipice of summer solstice.

Full moon rises
above wetland tules and mist.

Swollen orb
glows between sycamore limbs.

Dim light infiltrates darkened rooms,
inflames summer's sensual itch.

Wetland Cypress

Emerging from drifting fog
like a Frankenstein monster,
scarred arms splay
above sage, rusty chaparral.
Tiny fireworks blooms
of bright summer mustard.

Ground squirrels honeycomb
between gnarled roots,
excavate deep burrows, well-traveled tunnels.
In late afternoon sun
they sprawl upon weathered stump
of the battered tree's
long-toppled, neighboring cypress.

Wild turkeys scratch dusty verge.
Red-winged blackbirds dip and sway,
as they cling to silver leaf willows.
A hawk perches on the highest
cypress branch, surveys wetland
for fleeing mice, terrorized bunnies.

Cambria Ramble

Sharp eyed stellar jays
hear me lumbering up Bill Kerr Trail,
nervously flit to treetops,
sound an urgent alert.

Poison oak flares
scarlet from underbrush.
Scent of chipped pine logs
perfumes morning air.

Knotted roots bisect winding pathway.
After two recent tumbles,
I move deliberately, exercise caution,
tell myself this isn't a marathon,
more precisely, a dance.

Thistle

Gray fog billows ashore,
forms opaque backdrop to brittle thorns,
erases volcanic boulders.

With Salvador Dali mustache,
a dried thistle, denuded of downy seed,
restrains a honeybee.

Among mustard, wild radish,
still-green progeny burrs
erupt bright purple flowers.

Brambles provide barbed cover
for scrambling squirrels,
foraging field mice.

I wander Moonstone Beach.
Barbed stems bristle, rattle in the breeze.
Your ghost clings like prickly nettles.

Sunset at Leffingwell Landing

Afternoon sun melts toward surf.
Hot, dripping fireball
paints contorted oak limbs,
spills illumination
across restless waves.

Children squeal, sprint
downhill to secret sand bar,
leave behind a laboring woman
who struggles step to step.

I stand on high ground,
soak in summer warmth,
spiraling gulls, feathery blizzard,
sound of whispering surf,
savor the golden hour,
segue to ascending moon,
indigo nightfall.

Moonstone Morning

All night, surf calls, shaping sand,
eroding stone, with whispering fingers.

I hike boardwalk trail, share crumbling headlands
with morning walkers, jacketed dogs, a giant blue heron.

Wet-suited surfers pull themselves out to sea,
rock and wait, straddling surfboards.

Periwinkle and wild radish
ornament drab sage, native sedge.

Foamy breakers roll ashore.
Ghostly mist hangs above tangled seaweed, driftwood and feathers.

Drizzle

Triple digit Central Valley heat
pulls a foggy blanket over bleak shoreline,
fills silver skies with gloomy faux clouds.

Drizzle spatters parked cars,
streaks windowpanes, saturates
joggers' soggy jackets and shoes.

Sparrows delicately sip
from puddles beneath fuchsias.
Passing dogs flaunt damp fur, muddy paws.

Gray seaside summer impersonates winter,
obliterates sunlight as icy winds
blow inland, bite to the bone.

Camera Obscura

Shoreline vanishes, devoured by mist.
On a dead branch,
sodden turkey vultures sulk,
a dispirited trio.

I view morning through
smudgy scrim,
hike damp trail,
sharp edges softened.

Destination is fluid,
determined by blackberry bramble,
elevation of adobe bluff,
suspicious skunk blocking my path.

Sky and sea become one indistinct smear.
Blurry blue herons emerge and vanish.
Pelicans glide and drift.
Muffled surf rearranges raw stone.

Del Monte Beach

Silently, I ramble to rocking gray ocean
where squid trawlers drag steel jigs
through clotted schools of tentacled silver.

A phalanx of pelicans, circled by gulls,
observe squirming carnage,
swoop in for fishy spoils,
skim above orange paint brush,
pink sand verbena.

Wordlessly, I savor salt breeze,
sanctuary bay, this holy meditation
upon soul-piercing beauty.

Inhaling white sage perfume,
I admire steepled masts, barking harbor seals,
drifting red kayaks.

Morning Hike

Staccato birdsong
sprinkles itself
across oak forest canopy.

Underfoot, invisible creatures
skitter through shoals
of brittle rattlesnake grass.

As the anniversary
of mom's death approaches,
I walk through inchoate grief.

Pyrotechnic poison oak brambles
mark unsafe deviations
from traditional trail.

Acknowledgement of loss,
not summer allergies,
brings tears that streak my wet face.

Along golden ridge top,
icy winds blow inland,
ghosts of sullen gray sea.

I shiver, feel mortality's chilly hand
upon my shoulder, kindle gratitude for
morning hike, gift of an uncluttered day.

Acknowledgements

Thank you to Kate Aver Avraham, Laura Bayless, Diane Frank, Mary Kay Rummel and Patrice Vecchione for their editorial assistance and literary support.

Grateful acknowledgment is made to the following journals in which these poems have appeared, sometimes in different versions:

"White Fire of the Stars," *Speckled Trout Review*, Fall 2019

"Full Moon Over Sausalito," *Rockford Review*, Summer/Fall 2020

"Fall," *Creativity Webzine*, Issue 100, October 4, 2018.

"Smolder," *New Verse News*, August 19, 2016.

"Marina Dunes Preserve," *Nature Writing*, June 22, 2017.

"Harbor," *Poetrymagazine.com*, July 2017.

"Moon Fall," *GFT Presents: One in Four*, Vol. 1, Issue 2, Fall 2016.

"Descent," *Monterey Poetry Review*, Sept. 15, 2017.

"Beach Bon Mot," *Nature Writing*, May 15, 2017.

"Blue Heron," *Nature Writing*, June 9, 2017.

"Harvest Moon," *Song of the San Joaquin*, Volume XV, Number 4, Fall, 2018.

"Over the Moon," *Mystical Muse*, April 10, 2020.

"Sentinel," *Song of the San Joaquin*, Vol. 14, No. 2 (Spring 2017).

"Ripple Effect," *Mystical Muse*, April 10, 2020.

"On the Verge," *Mystical Muse*, April 10, 2020.

"Leffingwell Landing," *Nature Writing*, April 8, 2016.

"Fire in the Sky," *Nature Writing*, February 15, 2017.

"Fog Walker," *Nature Writing*, August 14, 2018.

"Atmospheric Disturbance," *Song of the San Joaquin*, Vol. XVI, No. 2, Spring 2019.

"Outlook," *Nature Writing*, May 20, 2016. "Misty Morning," *Nature Poetry*, May 28, 2016.

"Incoming," *GFT Presents: One in Four,* Vol. 2, Issue 1 (Spring 2017).

"Red Sky in Morning," *Naturewriting.com,* December 10, 2016.

"Homecoming," *Red Eft Review,* May 12, 2020.

"Maelstrom," *Song of the San Joaquin,* Vol. XVI, No. 2, Spring 2019.

"Epiphany," *Paterson Literary Review,* Issue 43, 2015-2016.

"Storm," *Song of the San Joaquin,* Vol. 14, No. 1 (Winter 2017).

"Rain Lullaby," *Song of the San Joaquin,* Vol. XVI, No. 3 (Summer 2019).

"Oxalis," *Song of the San Joaquin,* Vol. XV, No. 2, Spring 2018.

"Storm Clouds and Lupine, *Nature Writing,* July 26, 2016.

"Peach Blossoms," *GFT Presents: One in Four,* Vol. 1, Issue 1, Spring 2016.

"Night Music," *Nature Writing,* March 27, 2017.

"Monterey Marina," *Monterey Poetry Review,* Sept. 15, 2017.

"Spring Rainstorm," *Nature Writing,* April 28, 2017.

"Wildflower Ramble," *Nature Writing,* July 14, 2017.

"Gratitude," *Nature Writing,* May 25, 2017.

"Postcards of Light," *Song of the San Joaquin,* Vol. XVI, No. 3 (Summer 2019).

"Naked Ladies," *Song of the San Joaquin,* Vol. 16, No. 4, Fall 2019.

"Squirrel," *Nature Writing,* July 20, 2018.

"Frog Pond," *Poetrymagazine.com,* July 2017.

"Solstice Moon," *Song of the San Joaquin,* Vol. XIII, No. 4, Fall 2016.

"Wetland Cypress," *Nature Writing,* June 28, 2016.

"Thistle," *Naturewriting.com,* November 26, 2016.

"Drizzle," *Ravensperch,* July 24, 2017.

"Camera Obscura," *Nature Writing,* September 4, 2018.

About the Author

Dr. Jennifer Lagier has published eighteen books. Her work has appeared most recently in *From Everywhere a Little: A Migration Anthology, Fire and Rain: Ecopoetry of California, Missing Persons: Reflections on Dementia, Silent Screams: Poetic Journeys Through Addiction & Recovery, Winedrunk Sidewalk, I Am Not a Silent Poet, Song of the San Joaquin, Speckled Trout Review, Syndic Literary Journal.* Recent books: *Camille Verite* (FutureCycle Press), *Where We Grew Up* (FutureCycle Press), *Scene of the Crime* (Evening Street Press), *Harbingers* (Blue Light Press), *Camille Abroad* (FutureCycle Press), *Like a B Movie* (FutureCycle Press), *Camille Mobilizes* (FutureCycle Press), *Trumped Up Election* (Xi Draconis Books) , *Dystopia Playlist* (Cyberwit) and *Camille Comes Unglued* (Cyberwit). Links to her books and anthologies where her work appears may be found at jlagier.net/books.html and jlagier.net/anthologies.html

Jennifer earned a Ph.D. from Nova Southeastern University, an MLIS from University of California, Berkeley, and an MA from California State University, Stanislaus. She taught at Modesto Junior College, Hartnell College, California State University, Monterey Bay, and Monterey Peninsula College. She taught with California Poets in the Schools and edited the Homestead Review. Currently, she edits the *Monterey Poetry Review* and helps coordinate Second Sunday readings for the Monterey Poetry Consortium.

Visit her website: jlagier.net and her author's page on Facebook: www.facebook.com/JenniferLagier/

Books by Jennifer Lagier

Meditations on Seascapes and Cypress, Blue Light Press, 2021.

Camille Comes Unglued, Cyberwit, 2020.

Dystopia Playlist, Cyberwit, 2020.

Trumped Up Election, Xi Draconis Books, 2019.

Camille Mobilizes, FutureCycle Press, 2018.

Like a B Movie, FutureCycle Press, 2018.

Harbingers, Blue Light Press, 2016.

Scene of the Crime, Evening Street Press, 2016.

Camille Abroad, FutureCycle Press, 2016.

Where We Grew Up, FutureCycle Press, 2015.

Camille Vérité, FutureCycle Press, 2014.

Penetrating the Mist, Green Fuse Poetic Arts, 2013.

Hookup with Chinaski, Paisano Press, 2013.

Agent Provacateur, Paisano Press, 2012.

Fishing for Portents, Pudding House Publications, 2008.

Mangia Syndrome, Pudding House Publications, 2004.

Second-Class Citizen, Bordigheria, Inc., 2000.

Where We Grew Up, Paisano Press, 1999.

Coyote Dream Cantos, Iota Press, 1992.

www.ingramcontent.com/pod-product-compliance
Lightning Source LLC
Chambersburg PA
CBHW021343090426
42742CB00008B/732